First published by Walker Books Ltd in
Bear's Birthday (1985), *Big Bad Pig* (1985),
Happy Worm (1985), *Look out for the Seals!* (1986)
and *Make a Face* (1985)

This edition published 1995

2 4 6 8 10 9 7 5 3 1

Text © 1985, 1986 Allan Ahlberg
Illustrations © 1985, 1986 Colin McNaughton

This book has been typeset in ITC Garamond Light.

Printed in Italy

British Library Cataloguing in Publication Data
A catalogue record for this book is
available from the British Library.
ISBN 0-7445-3738-X

PUT ON A SHOW!

Allan Ahlberg + Colin McNaughton

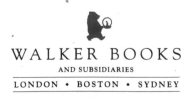

WALKER BOOKS
AND SUBSIDIARIES
LONDON • BOSTON • SYDNEY

open the
door

shut the
door

open the
window

shut the
window

open the
fridge

shut the
fridge

open the box

shut the box

open the parcel

11

SPOTTY DOG

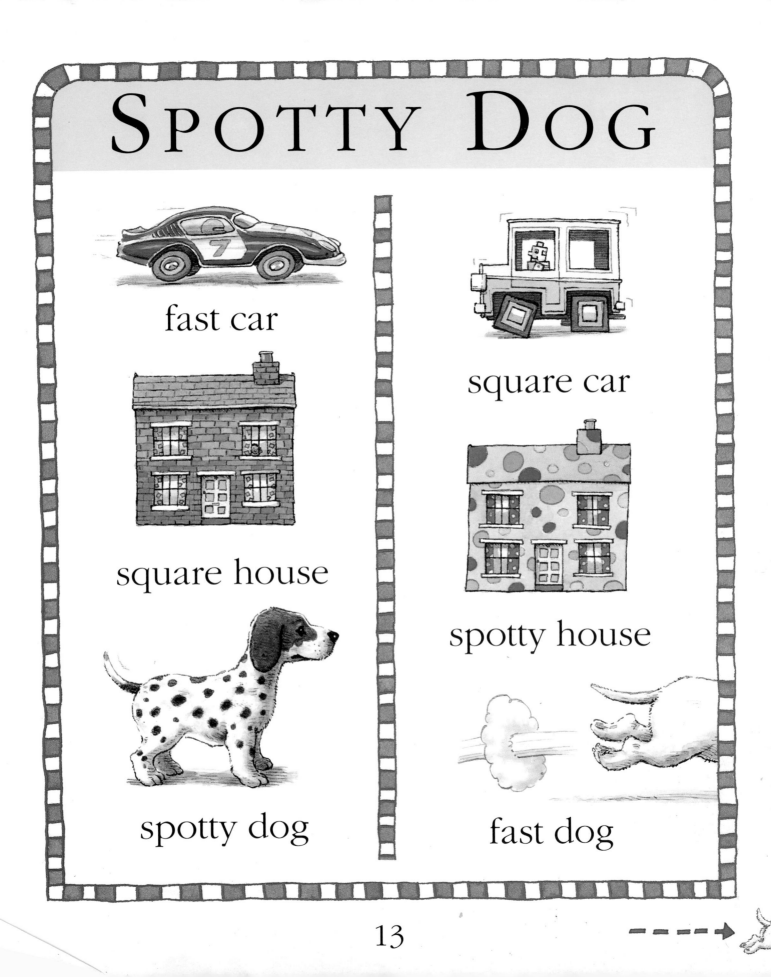

fast car

square car

square house

spotty house

spotty dog

fast dog

fast house

before the witch

after the witch

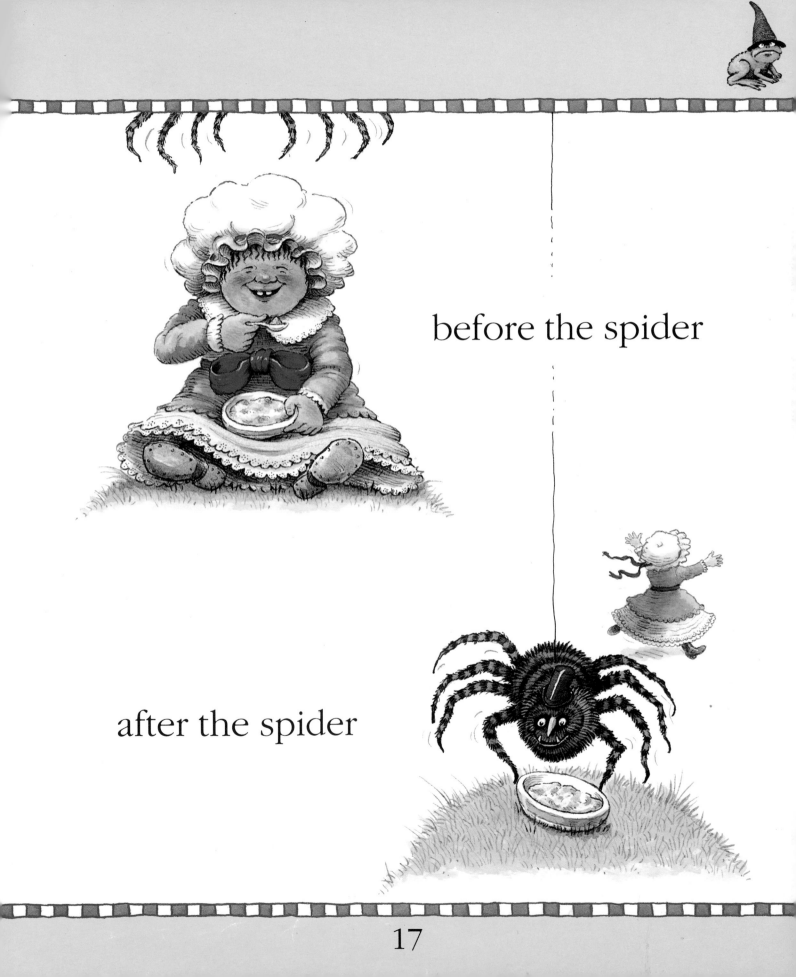

before the spider

after the spider

before the wolf

after the wolf

LOST CAT

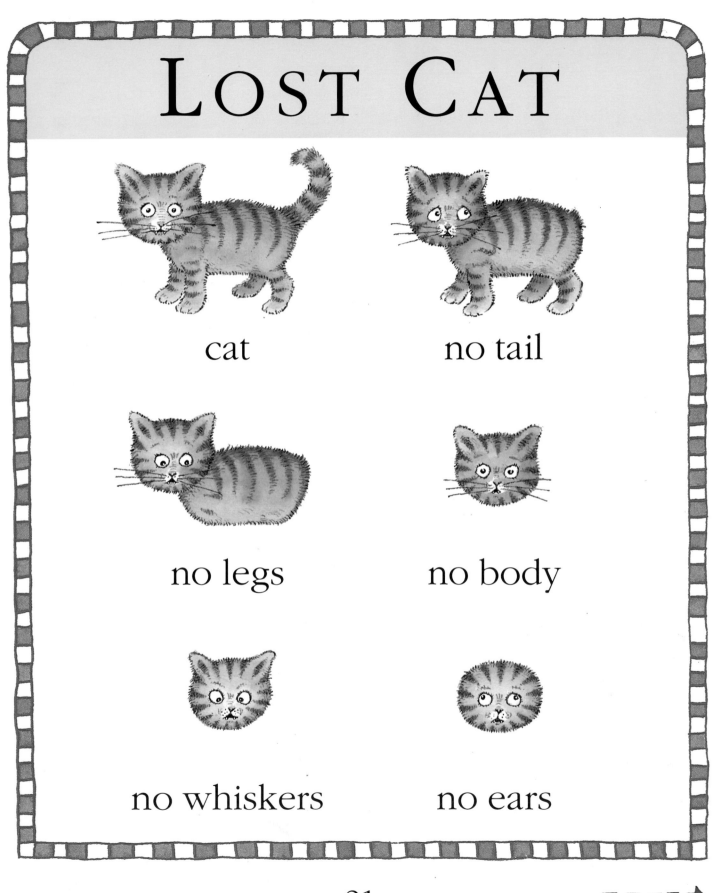

cat

no tail

no legs

no body

no whiskers

no ears

no cat

a happy worm

a sad worm

a happy bird

a sad bird

a happy cat

a sad cat

a happy dog

a sad dog

a happy dog

FROG

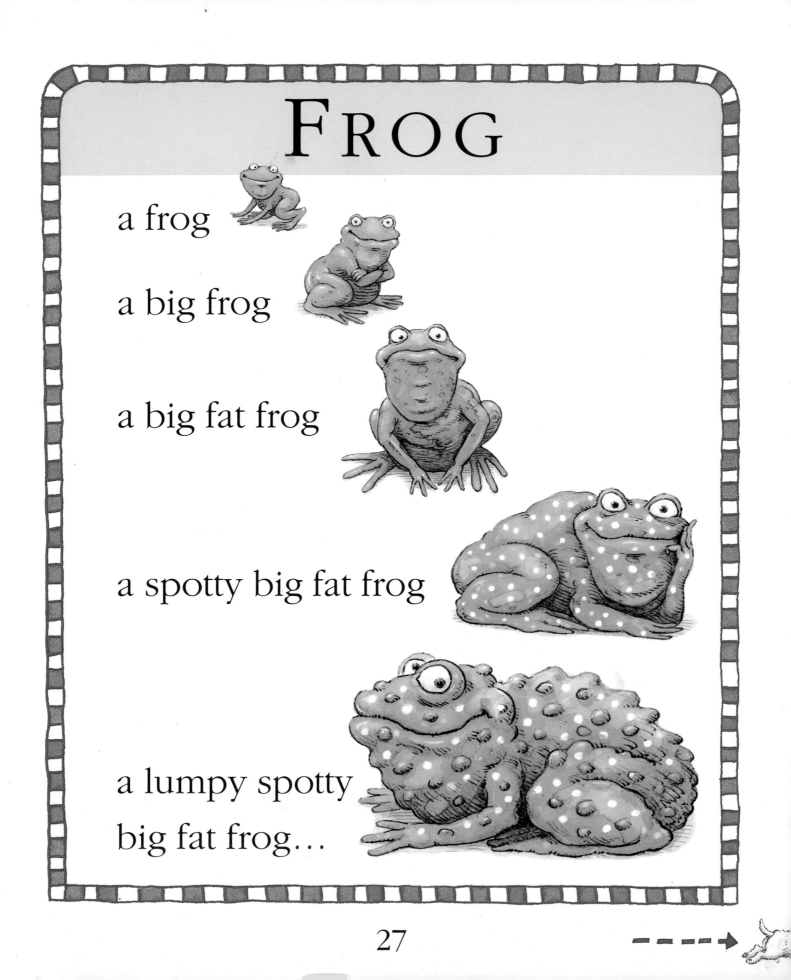

a frog

a big frog

a big fat frog

a spotty big fat frog

a lumpy spotty
big fat frog…

...with a hat on

LOOK OUT FOR THE SEALS!

Here is the house,
the doors are open wide,
so step this way,
come right inside.

– Look out for the seals!

This is the hall
full of potted plants,
umbrellas, boots –
and elephants!

– What are *they* doing here?

Here is the maid,
her name is Mabel,
giving a shine to
the dining table.

– She's a hard
worker.

Here is the kitchen,
here is the cook,
baking bread
and reading a book.

– And lighting the fire, too!

Up the stairs,
mind how you go,
there's a man coming
down with a buffalo.

– It's a young buffalo,
by the look of it.

Here on the landing the Mighty Keith
is lifting a wardrobe with his teeth.

– He can lift two wardrobes, when he has to.

This bedroom is full, I expect you can tell,
there are cowboys in here and horses as well.

– The Indians are in the bathroom.

Here in the attic a couple of boys
are messing about
with their sister's toys.

– As you can see, *she* doesn't like it.

Down in the garden a man and his twin
are helping to get the washing in.

– Their friend *isn't* helping.

Back on the landing the Mighty Keith
is lifting a *buffalo* with his teeth.

– Looks like he dropped the wardrobe, though.

Down the stairs, look – here's the maid
with fancy cakes and lemonade!

– Are these for *us*, Mabel?

Now at last it's time to go.

(Look out for the seals!)

Next time you come we'll…

Put on

the end